CW00728218

Published by and printed through Amazon 2022

ISBN: 9798409568351

To Amanda Stephens
May 10 words always be enough

Contents   **Page**

Poetry Categories

As a novice poet, I joined an online site, which is where I met Jaden. It was time for me to grow as a writer and when I began reading his poetry, it was easy for me to see that I could learn a lot from him.

From his rhyme to his 3-liners which always give me reason to pause and think - he is one of the poets I chose to "follow" so I could develop.   My decision to follow him has helped me grow as a poet and as a person.

Because we've become friends through poetry, I can confidently say that I have learnt so much from him and it is possible that you might too.

He is a great poet, teacher and friend and I hope you enjoy his second book.

Lou Ammerman, "Lou Woodfae"

Welcome to my second book of poetry.

From a young age I enjoyed playing with words and although it was not always appreciated, I still had fun with the results.

Writing can be an enormous release for me as thoughts and feelings can be buried onto a page instead of being bottled up inside of my mind. I like to write to rebel against the illusion and the lie that there is such a thing as a "normal" person, and to have my own fun.

I wrote my first three lined piece as an experiment before realising how much fun they were to write and so I continued. I had no idea how much the idea of them would catch on in my mind and become so useful to me.

Whether you laugh, cry or just scratch your head in disbelief, I hope you have as much fun reading these as I have writing them.

Jaden Knight

Fun With Food

Large White And Fluffy

Large white and fluffy
swinging to and from desserts
the mering-utang

The Comedy Eggs

The comedy eggs
love to be cooked in a pan
fried funny side up

Viking Cannibal

Viking cannibal
says he's vegetarian
will only eat swedes

Some Oranges Talk

Some oranges talk
while growing on their trees
they speak mandarin

Potato Music

Potato music
is very boring to hear
they play the tuber

Broken Colander

Broken colander
it's feeling down and hopeless
lost the will to sieve

Puddings Leave Army

Puddings leave army
face a court martial hearing
they tried to dessert

Made A Lamb Korma

Made a lamb korma
to impress a lady friend
am currying favour

Vegetable Pipes

Vegetable pipes
designed to carry water
now have sprung a leek

Some Breads Can Act Well

Some breads can act well
and star on the silver screen
playing any rolls

Spuds In A Deep Trance

Spuds in a deep trance
trying to escape the pan
they're medi-taters

Argument With Steak

Argument with steak
keeps shouting accusations
got serious beef

A Squash Ate Too Much

A squash ate too much
becoming round and orange
friends call it plump-kin

Have Captured Cream Cakes

Have captured cream cakes
will cut them all into thirds
no quarter given

Almonds In Deep Space

Almonds in deep space
bouncing around the shuttle
floating astro-nuts

Dried Grape As Queen

Dried grape as queen
of giant desert nation
powerful Sultana

Beautiful Nature

Large Seagull Dances

Large seagull dances
on empty picnic tables
waiting for next meal

Black cat Slowly Stretches

Black cat slowly stretches
and begins her daily prowl
tonight's hunt is on

Honey Bees Buzzing

Honey bees buzzing
lots of nectar to gather
work never finished

Magnificent Stag

Magnificent stag
his huge antlers are his crown
king of all he sees

A Young Fawn Suckles

A young fawn suckles
feasting on its mother's milk
mum keeps watch for wolves

Happy Kittens Play

Happy kittens play
brother and sister fighting
learning and growing

Young Cygnet Prince Swims

Young cygnet prince swims
heir to his father's kingdom
ducklings give him space

Sheep Graze Happily

Sheep graze happily
bleating between their mouthfuls
shepherd is asleep

Black Cat Is Digging

Black cat is digging
her sharp claws into my legs
looking for comfort

Seagulls Soar Above

Seagulls soar above
looking for an easy meal
guard your sandwiches

Playful Lamb Bounces

Playful lamb bounces
around its grazing mother
watched by hungry wolf

Silverback Patrols

Silverback patrols
dense trees of his jungle home
his troop sleep in peace

Geese Are Flying North

Geese are flying north
migrating in formation
spring is on its way

White Eggs Start Cracking

White eggs start cracking
tiny chicks escape their shells
hen watches proudly

Wild Horses Gallop

Wild horses gallop
through the tall desert grasses
play time for the foals

Young Lion Cubs Play

Young lion cubs play
learning with every tumble
practising their skills

Funny Animals

Primate Does Forecast

Primate does forecast
floating way up near the clouds
a weather baboon

Elks Leave Messages

Elks leave messages
for their friends and family
they're using moose code

A Clumsy Dolphin

A clumsy dolphin
does most things by accident
never on porpoise

Hedgehog Fought A Mouse

Hedgehog fought a mouse
it was a vicious punch up
decided on points

Sheep Composers Fight

Sheep composers fight
over just how many bleats
should be in a baa

Giant Duck Spreads Fear

Giant duck spreads fear
bringing destruction and death
beware the Quacken

Penguin Given Bail

Penguin given bail
lawyer convinced the judges
he isn't a flight risk

Psychic Termite Group

Psychic termite group
able to predict future
they are clairvoy-ants

Met A Cat Today

Met a cat today
he is radioactive
has eighteen half lives

Tried Paying Rhinos

Tried paying rhinos
it got very expensive
they charged far too much

Mallard Plays Cricket

Mallard plays cricket
loses his stumps on first ball
he's out for a duck

Bee Sells Its Honey

Bee sells its honey
twenty dollars for a jar
sting operation

Skunk Feels It's Broken

Skunk feels it's broken
cannot release its foul scent
it's out of odour

Terrapins Don't Drink

Terrapins don't drink
despising all alcohol
they are tee-turtle

Mollusc Sighs Aloud

Mollusc sighs aloud
and opens his umbrella
clam before the storm

Giant Wasps Invade

Giant wasps invade
Yellowstone national park
swat team has been called

Help An Octopus

Help an octopus
and they'll return the favour
they do squid pro quo

Most Hamsters Can't Drive

Most hamsters can't drive
too many have been spotted
asleep at the wheel

Got A New Mouse Mat

Got a new mouse mat
have put it by my window
rats now wipe their feet

Swimming With Wild Sharks

Swimming with wild sharks
is normally expensive
costs an arm and leg

Seasonal Joy

Snowflakes Kiss The Ground

Snowflakes kiss the ground
love between the ground and sky
a winter romance

Spring Is Demanded

Spring is demanded
winter wastefully spent
but summer is earned

Cruel Winter Invades

Cruel winter invades
sending forth armies of snow
armed with bitter winds

Summer Surrenders

Summer surrenders
its tired soldiers shed their leaves
autumn brings defeat

The Snowflakes Swirl

The snowflakes swirl
like butterflies of winter
dancing in the wind

Flurries Of Snow Fall

Flurries of snow fall
temperature tumbles
winter's grip squeezes

Spring Growth Was Shooting

Spring growth was shooting
with a brand-new camera
grass was directing

Yellow flames flicker

Yellow flames flicker
as if blown by hidden drafts
Halloween candles

Joy Blooms With Flowers

Joy blooms with flowers
wonder of spring time healing
blossoms bring me hope

Let Silver Bells Ring

Let silver bells ring
announcing the festive news
Christmas is coming

White Shores Are Calling

White shores are calling
time for a dream holiday
paradise awaits

Icing Sugar Falls

Icing sugar falls
like snow on winter's morning
ginger bread men dance

Winter In Retreat

Winter in retreat
icy weather beaten back
spring's warmth advances

Spring Brings Its Healing

Spring brings its healing
chance for a positive start
closing winter's wounds

Autumn Starts Its Dance

Autumn starts its dance
dying leaves twirl as they fall
wind provides the tune

Summer Brings Heatwaves

Summer brings heatwaves
temperatures climb high
people wilt like plants

Friendship and Love

We Were Once Dreamers

We were once dreamers
sharing visions of the world
now you won't wake up

You'll Be In My Dreams

You'll be in my dreams
long after you leave this world
always on my mind

I Hope To See You

I hope to see you
waiting for me at the gates
tail wagging with joy

Sweet Love's Flower Blooms

Sweet love's flower blooms
a delicate blood red rose
I'm your honey bee

My Day Became A Night

My day became a night
your sun left my horizon
dark thoughts are settling

She Glides Like A Swan

She glides like a swan
across the tiled ballroom floor
a queen of the dance

You Are A Jewel

You are a jewel
in the gold crown of friendship
shining like a star

Small Hummingbird Flies

Small hummingbird flies
giving me reasons to live
her wings my heartbeat

Tripped Over My Tongue

Tripped over my tongue
trying to say I love you
clumsy in romance

Sapphire Butterfly

Sapphire butterfly
continuing to inspire
long may she fly high

Wings Of Love Spread Wide

Wings of love spread wide
carry me across the seas
back into your arms

She Is A Lighthouse

She is a lighthouse
shining through the darkest night
a beacon of hope

I Can Be The Sun

I can be the sun
to your depression's full moon
feelings are eclipsed

Her Lips Were Cherries

Her lips were cherries
in both their colour and taste
could kiss them for hours

You Are like the Dawn

You are like the dawn
your sun rises in my world
drying tears of rain

My Ear Is Open

My ear is open
all you need to do is talk
and I will listen

Eyes Of Chocolate

Eyes of chocolate
diamond personality
loving heart of gold

I Offer You My Heart

I offer you my heart
gift-wrapped within my being
not just for Christmas

Three Flawless Diamonds

Three flawless diamonds
set in a platinum ring
a sign of my love

You'll Be In My Dreams

You'll be in my dreams
long after you leave this world
always on my mind

Life And Laughter

Threatened By Gold Bar

Threatened by gold bar
demanded all my money
it just loves bullion

Bullied Walking Stick

Bullied walking stick
stole one of its shoes
now it only hops

Stole An Air Guitar

Stole an air guitar
from an old friend of mine's room
he hasn't noticed yet

Am Blind In My Nose

Am blind in my nose
my eyes are completely deaf
my ears can't smell you

She Wielded Perfume

She wielded perfume
like a scent sledgehammer
my nose is broken

Girl Swallowed Magnet

Girl swallowed magnet
hoping it will change her looks
she's not attractive

Got New Camera

Got new camera
positively digital
got no negatives

Hunting For Lost Wheels

Hunting for lost wheels
stolen from my brand-new car
I work tyrelessly

Was Given a Map

Was given a map
of all the stars in the sky
constellation prize

Dated A Baker

Dated a baker
but it could never last long
she was too kneady

Robbed A Minstrel

Robbed a minstrel
and sold all his instruments
couldn't hide the lute

Bought A Light Aircraft

Bought a light aircraft
parked at a small aerodrome
they kept the hanger

Walked Into A Shop

Walked into a shop
with a big stick in my hand
got a staff discount

Memory Has Gone

Memory has gone
they say it's amnesia
maybe I forget

Judge Wasn't Happy

Judge wasn't happy
I took my lawyer to court
winning in straight sets

My Alarm Clock Shouts

My alarm clock shouts
swearing each time it goes off
rude awakening

Letters For Asgard

Letters for Asgard
prayers from ancient Vikings
written in Norse code

Went To Draw My Sword

Went to draw my sword
my best pencil won't sharpen
have to use a pen

Plane Misbehaving

Plane misbehaving
not doing what it is told
it's now been grounded

Went Out With A Carp

Went out with a carp
she was shy during dinner
acting very Koi

Night And Nature

Night Round The Fire Pit

Night round the fire pit
toasting marshmallows with friends
evenings of the past

Sun Gets Out Of Bed

Sun gets out of bed
rays lighting up the dark sky
dawn of a new day

The Moon Sings Alone

The moon sings alone
but no one hears her sweet songs
falling as soft light

Dawn Chorus Sounds Loud

Dawn chorus sounds loud
night was lost to poetry
writer is not tired

I Will be Your Moon

I will be your moon
in the darkest of nightmares
shining through your clouds

Sunset Tells Secrets

Sunset tells secrets
whispered from the fading rays
hiding from the night

Musical Weather

Musical weather
thunder provides the vocals
rain is on the drums

Hedgehog Feasts Tonight

Hedgehog feasts tonight
a worm is banquet laid out
beneath a rose bush

A Full Moon Rises

A full moon rises
silver wolves are on the hunt
bats fly overhead

Sunset Tells Secrets

Sunset tells secrets
whispered from the fading rays
hiding from the night

Tawny Owl Hoots Loud

Tawny owl hoots loud
tiny mice scurry in fear
rabbits hide away

Dog Sleeps By The Fire

Dog sleeps by the fire
paws twitching in running dreams
chasing hares again

Moths Dance Under Stars

Moths dance under stars
to music of cicadas
moon provides the lights

Barn Owl Glides Tonight

Barn owl glides tonight
a living ghost in the dark
hunting for field mice

The Moon Feels No Joy

The moon feels no joy
she only feels the sorrow
of being alone

Bats Wake At Sunset

Bats wake at sunset
stretching their leathery wings
they'll leave at twilight

Dead And Undead

Angry Poltergeist

Angry poltergeist
throws objects for attention
none can hear him cry

Undead Work On Ships

Undead work on ships
where no one else is willing
a skeleton crew

Mummies Get Very Stressed

Mummies get very stressed
bandages on far too tight
they need to unwind

Skeleton Robbers

Skeleton robbers
famous undead criminals
given life in jail

Zombie Has Gone Blind

Zombie has gone blind
it was caught rolling its eyes
crows have stolen them

Lich Casts His Foul Spells

Lich casts his foul spells
his chains remain unbroken
crypt his prison cell

Wimpy Skeleton

Wimpy skeleton
Wanted to do something brave
hasn't got the guts

Mummies Learn Banking

Mummies learn banking
use their tombs to earn money
a pyramid scheme

Melancholy Skull

Melancholy skull
he gets constantly ignored
no body listens

An Undead Locksmith

An undead locksmith
making new skeleton keys
hands worn to the bone

Amorous Mummies

Amorous mummies
kissing and more in public
need to get a tomb

Vampire Hit By Beef

Vampire hit by beef
gets killed almost instantly
a steak to the head

Vampires Cannot Field

Vampires cannot field
but enjoy playing baseball
they know how to bat

Undead Abe Lincoln

Undead Abe Lincoln
just bought a nice new mansion
Gettysburg address

Mummy Has Its Kinks

Mummy has its kinks
normally in the bedroom
it's into bandage

Zombie Footballer

Zombie footballer
shows off his skills with his head
ravens give applause

Impossible Images

Flamingo Pencils

Flamingo pencils
grow lemon grass potatoes
painting joyful smiles

Alligators Fly

Alligators fly
three robins swim in the ice
fish have gone walking

Cats Sprout Silver Wings

Cats sprout silver wings
pheasants march on bananas
sharks polish their knees

Three Zombie Limes Swim

Three zombie limes swim
lawnmower seeks to catch them
violet horse escapes

Frog Diamonds Grow Cakes

Frog diamonds grow cakes
penguin lions arrest socks
gloves build an orange

Light Bulb Eels Burn Socks

Light bulb eels burn socks
magnetic onions hunt spoons
daisies make glasses

Eagle Chins Paint Socks

Eagle chins paint socks
football boots make calendars
bottles cook eel forks

Plate Curtains Drink Chairs

Plate curtains drink chairs
table shoes knit dolphin wings
rose becomes a lime

Cat Cleans Up Pet Hair

Cat cleans up pet hair
dog does a child's homework
mouse sings lullabies

Parsnip Meerkats Swim

Parsnip meerkats swim
dolphin carrots chew on boats
onion sheep are robbed

Plum Egg Submarine

Plum egg submarine
caught in a blue onion sheep
ear shoes run away

Kitten Whales Surf Bears

Kitten whales surf bears
flying melon parrot sheep
digging for egg clouds

Artichoke Ears Hatch

Artichoke ears hatch
shells of whisky grow their fangs
ice tongues run away

Mice Are Hunting Eggs

Mice are hunting eggs
red lemons hide in terror
soap ice-cream burns

Table Was Pregnant

Table was pregnant
gave birth to a blue otter
eating purple fire

T Rex Owns Gun Shop

T rex owns gun shop
sells pistols to most people
a small arms dealer

Rose Bush Stole A Car

Rose bush stole a car
waving at termite penguins
salmon smokes a beer

Fox Wasp Lemon Sheep

Fox wasp lemon sheep
knit chocolate flame throwers
to freeze lava limes

Light Bulb Eels Burn Socks

Light bulb eels burn socks
magnetic onions hunt spoons
daisies make glasses

Llama Apples Sing

Llama apples sing
frightening dream giraffe fans
horseshoes swim away

Personal Projections

Aspergers Writers

Aspergers writers
are just very different
we are not broken

My Strings Are Broken

My strings are broken
I am my own Pinocchio
your puppet no more

Dancing In The Storm

Dancing in the storm
rain providing the applause
car park is my stage

You Won't See Me Cry

You won't see me cry
as I kick you out my life
only joyful smiles

Let Me Remain Lost

Let me remain lost
hidden in the thick black fog
don't try to find me

Call Me The Nomad

Call me the nomad
I don't belong anywhere
wandering through life

Not Your Stepping Stone

Not your stepping stone
I'll tip you in the river
don't try to use me

Am Learning Slowly

Am learning slowly
with almost snail like progress
still moving forward

My Mind Is A Cloud

My mind is a cloud
raining ideas on paper
hoping they will grow

Sunk My Battle Ship

Sunk my battle ship
when we weren't even playing
vessel of love lost

Brain Sings Happily

Brain sings happily
lungs provide the music
heart beats the tempo

No One Judges Me

No one judges me
in the way you do most days
my dear reflection

My Bed Is Calling

My bed is calling
but I'm on another phone
line always engaged

Am Out Of My Mind

Am out of my mind
time of return is unknown
please leave a message

Looked In The Mirror

Looked in the mirror
seen the reflections echoing
which one would be me

Eyes Speak Their Language

Eyes speak their language
to anyone who will listen
saying much without words

I Can't Be Normal

I can't be normal
can only be who I am
was born different

I Still Remember

I still remember
deep in my memory halls
your words keep echoing

I'm My Own Compass

I'm my own compass
refusing to point to north
I go my own way

I Have Concrete Ears

I have concrete ears
can't listen to anything
am hard of hearing

All About Alliteration

Flighty Flamingos

Flighty flamingos
gargle golden grapefruit grass
to train tired turtles

Piccolo Puffins

Piccolo puffins
pick pink pineapple peppers
praising punk puppies

Blue Badgers Build Books

Blue badgers build books
reading red regal roses
grow gorilla gloves

Chinchilla Chainsaws

Chinchilla chainsaws
hunt hammerhead hummingbirds
fire fish feet feed frogs

Shiny Seagull Sharks

Shiny seagull sharks
surf sandwich submarine shoes
selling silver seals

Penguin Pencils Pray

Penguin pencils pray
seeking solitude sandwiches
tripping trumpet tins

Ant Apples Abseil

Ant apples abseil
humming helicopters hatch
dizzy dogfish dance

Camouflaged Camels

Camouflaged camels
create custard catapults
causing catfish cars

Pirate Penguins Paint

Pirate penguins paint
luminous lime lions laughing
at ant apple arms

Custard Cat Crabs Cry

Custard cat crabs cry
curried cathodes catch cars
crushed carbon cans crawl

Brontosaurus Basks

Brontosaurus basks
behind barking ball baskets
bowling blind badgers

Saxophone Seagulls

Saxophone seagulls
crash cuttlefish carrot cogs
for foxglove ferrets

Tuna Toes Tango

Tuna toes tango
to teak tomato tunes
tracing trombone trains

Custard Comet Cats

Custard comet cats
painted by peg pianos
numb noses nightly

Marmalade Monsters

Marmalade monsters
melt mahogany mincemeat
making mint muffins

Brilliant Brass Bulls Bounce

Brilliant brass bulls bounce
broken beaver bread branches
biting blue bottles

Green Glass Geese Gallop

Green glass geese gallop
on onion omelette ore
chasing cocoa cats

Crying Crayon Crumbs

Crying crayon crumbs
colour copper cats crimson
concrete caps call coats

Piccolo Panthers

Piccolo panthers
parade pregnant pelicans
pecan plums plotting

Stegosaurus Steps

Stegosaurus steps
vex violent violins
lion lunches laugh

Random Thoughts

Turn The Page My Dear

Turn the page my dear
let the words breathe and take root
deep inside your mind

A Man Is Not Dead

A man is not dead
while others still speak his name
alive in memories

My Words Are Sprouting

My words are sprouting
growing from poetry's ash
threatening to bloom

The Pen Is A Sword

The pen is a sword
cutting through the ignorance
knowledge bleeds through ink

Life Has Its Prices

Life has its prices
everything we say and do
will have its own costs

Words Can Cut Deeper

Words can cut deeper
than any known knife or sword
causing hidden scars

Congregation Quiet

Congregation quiet
Father offers his blessing
silver bells ring out

Pull The Bowstring Taut

Pull the bowstring taut
Aim for the distant target
Let the arrow fly

You Be The Paper

You be the paper
I can be the loving pen
writing out our thoughts

Poetic Fire Burns

Poetic fire burns
fuelled by darkest memories
burning them away

My Mind Is A Cloud

My mind is a cloud
raining ideas on paper
hoping they will grow

Words Are Raining Down

Words are raining down
a monsoon of poetry
rivers of verse formed

Poetic Surfer

Poetic surfer
Rides the creative waves home
their pen is their board

Print Is Not Dead Ink

Print is not dead ink
it can still live happily
in a reader's mind

Thought Battering Ram

Thought battering ram
breaking walls of ignorance
knowledge will conquer

Gold Is Never Good

Gold is never good
corrupting both hearts and minds
feeding only greed

Revenge Is So Sweet

Revenge is so sweet
just like a bowl of ice cream
it is best served cold

Child Of The Cosmos

Child of the cosmos
wishes she could return home
sparkling with the stars

Ideas Are Coal

Ideas are coal
for the engine of my mind
keeps pistons moving

We Should Be Like Streams

We should be like streams
always progressing forward
never flowing back

Miscellaneous Mirth

Our Solar System

Our solar system
poorly rated by aliens
only has one star

Poetry In Jails

Poetry in jails
to educate inmates
it has prose and cons

New Electric Store

New electric store
sells mostly resistors
called ohm depot

Hamlet Of Socks

Hamlet of socks
feared by almost everyone
village of the darned

Fell Into Snow Globe

Fell into snow globe
ended up with huge bruises
was badly shaken

Old broken Records

Old broken records
buried under the oak trees
vinyl resting place

Plane Misbehaving

Plane misbehaving
not doing what it is told
it's now been grounded

Eighteen Carrot Gold

Eighteen carrot gold
bought by a rich jeweller
eaten by rabbits

Jigsaws Don't Want War

Jigsaws don't want war
violence is not their way
they come in pieces

Mouse Has Gone Missing

Mouse has gone missing
laptop won't work without it
the cat has been blamed

Broom Becomes Mayor

Broom becomes mayor
promises change on first day
plans sweeping reforms

Broken Telescope

Broken telescope
is so awful at its job
it cannot focus

Too Much Resistance

Too much resistance
trying to push through cables
am going back ohm

Old Tank Ticks And Swears

Old tank ticks and swears
claims medical condition
says it has turrets

An Eight Limbed Surgeon

An eight limbed surgeon
has too many hands and feet
he's a doctor-puss

A Pirate Boxer

A pirate boxer
he's almost undefeated
has vicious left hook

Fight Over Scrabble

Fight over scrabble
ended in very bad way
someone lost an I

Crazy Wooden Horse

Crazy wooden horse
needs urgent mental treatment
he's off his rocker

Thinking Of Cables

Thinking of cables
mostly of copper and steel
but I don't know wire

Some Nails Drink Too Much

Some nails drink too much
while sitting in their tool boxes
many get hammered

Acknowledgements

I would like to start off by thanking Stephanie and Amanda for accidentally setting me the challenge for the 3 liners. It looks like I succeeded in completing winning the challenge so far and hopefully will continue to do so.

Boo for almost being the older brother that I never had the chance to have. His straight forward attitude inspires me and while he does not have his own piece yet I am sure that it will be written soon.

Anna and Richard for being a family away from family. Though they are always very busy they are happy to make time for me and I am always grateful for their assistance.

Cynthia and Sky for being part of a long-distance family. I may not be a proud and beautiful potato like you but I appreciate your support and hugs.

Gergana for providing honest feedback and a couple of minor suggestions. A couple have grown into something much more and hopefully ideas will continue to bloom.

Lou Woodfae for being there at almost all times of the day to check I am ok. You have been very patient with me over the last 4 years even when I have not been at my best and I very much appreciate your presence.

Jed for being so patient with me in the past when being read poetry. Sadly, you never got to hear or see any of the 3 liners that feature here but I am sure you would have listened patiently as I read them to you even if you would not have offered any criticism or opinion on them.

Ariel and Marie for their useful advice and ideas. I may not be the strong blue butterfly that you both are but I can still look up to you as you soar high above.

Doug for his opinions on the 3 liners I have shown him. Always seems to have time for me and have a laugh despite being 4,000 plus miles away.

To those who I have clashed blades with (both friend and foe) for giving me the weapons and ammunition. Though you may or may not be important enough to name you still made a contribution even if it was by accident

Printed in Great Britain
by Amazon

82409068R00047